Once Upon a Riot

Once Upon a Riot

poems

Dawn Tefft

Chicago | Los Angeles

Once Upon a Riot

Copyright © 2025 by Dawn Tefft

Published in the United States by Match Factory Editions, 2025

ISBN 978-1-966253-07-5 (hardcover)
ISBN 978-1-966253-06-8 (paperback)
ISBN 978-1-966253-08-2 (ebook)

Library of Congress Control Number: 2025931335

matchfactoryeditions.com

Book layout by RD Morgan

Cover art and design by Gretchen Hasse

Colophon design by Randy Cochran

For Ana, who I love with all my heart.
Your joy and love have brightened my life immeasurably.

For a better future for all, whether we know them or not.

...whenever a lot of money comes together in just one hand it's always a kind of robbery of the rest of us.

— Miguel Ángel Asturias, *Men of Maize*

If we do not now dare everything, the fulfillment of that prophecy, re-created from the Bible in song by a slave, is upon us: God gave Noah the rainbow sign. No more water, fire next time.

— James Baldwin, *The Fire Next Time*

Heart:

make yourself known here too
here, in the middle of the market.
Call out the shibboleth
away from home:
February. No pasaran.

— Paul Celan, "Schibboleth"

"It's times like these when it's easy to start thinking Nature could have had a better design," I said. "Like, for instance, that babies' bones would form after birth, instead of before. That would mean you could just ooze them out."

When I told her that, she brightened a little. But logic forced another thought, and I added, "But then you'd have to carry them around in a mixing bowl for a while so their bones could develop."

She laughed about what an unsatisfactory situation that would be. With her next push-pain, she got down and pushed and soon had her baby.

— *Ina May's Guide to Childbirth*

Table of Contents

I.

L&D

They came at me with a tube
a way to get inside of me and watch

They were always wanting to see

Each baby an experiment

Each mother a thump and whir
and whack

Sure, there was something to try
and save inside of something else
to try and save, but there was also
a technology of bodies

a mechanic can only be a mechanic
if there are mechanics to work out

prelude to each consent
(to be imagined as a refrain):
repeated attempts to convince
repeated stern faces

a trail of bloody water starting at the bed
a message without content
read differently by each party

converging and diverging points
of interest while an ocean
continued to ocean itself

we were here to figure something

September 8, 2018

The photo looks like Vermeer
everything muted colors
except your perfect body
being lifted up toward the light
a thin red cord stretching below

Home / Shelter / View

two lit windows across the way and a scream
        from a child below

              door bells ringing in my apartment
                  and the apartments all around me

                  a masked neighbor touches our shared
                      door knob on the gate to the lot

I say, "you go first, just let it slam, that way I don't breathe on you"

                      two blocks away, the lake
                          has taken what it wants

            water covers the beaches and sidewalks
                all the way up to the painted benches

my toddler tries to run into the lake
            where it overtakes the path and the prairie grass

                  people in masks take photos and videos
                    to show it really did erode overnight

we all gawk six feet apart
        while my daughter shovels sand
            where there should be concrete

                  when I get home, more emails
                    saying workers need ER visits covered

and my daughter draws me an endless spiral

                      meanwhile, all the normal emergencies
                           continue to accrue

as people eat too much sugar and
        continue to drink to the point of black outs

           today my mother called to say
                someone shot off my brother's ear

When I Win, I Start Again

with my one wild and precious
I am compelled to press
start over and over

why must I dive into the cleft
sit with my *Schneepart*

come up with a mouthful of
I did it wrong

consult the cards looking
for Empress in the new year

or at least The Fool at the start
of the month

why can I not find the place
where the route snakes
forward

see the strategy of the maps
I spread across the office
the way I decorate a couch
or raise my daughter
to jump on a trampoline
how the earth shakes
when I pronounce *no pasarán*
to mean *the fascists will die*
in the mountain pass
and when spring comes

it comes with new songs
touch the underside
of just about any valley
so that it moans with today
and is not merely a site
all that history is is
how you arrived here

My Daughter Sleeps with the Lights Dimmed

just enough to illuminate the outlines
of shapes and colors, of what is

helicopters fly overhead, dispatched
to survey, or save, or quell

rich men continue to invent
ways of consolidating their power

she rides whatever waves of birds and mama
and oatmeal and traffic and song

the scary and beautiful news of the city
country, world spells itself out

in faint symbology of crops and regimes
teachers and small regional kindnesses

the world narrows down to the rise
and fall of a chest in a milk-scented room

The Ongoing Work of Liberation,
Or the Aggressiveness of Liberation Theology

your skinned knees
I've never seen you bleed before

I hold you while you cry
and then you get down and run
and fall and run and fall again

a way to unfuck democracy

you try to join every volleyball
or soccer game we pass

I pick you up and carry you screaming

architectural details minus
content is merely mechanical

it doesn't matter that the bricks
are made from mud dredged
from Lake Calumet

or that the factory is in ruins

it says a lot that there's a memorial
rose garden for a strike

that workers were paid
minus the rent for row houses

and your skin is blooming
with crusty roses

because you see yourself
everywhere you can't wait to get

Nashville's Court House Is Burning

I turn on the TV to learn more
about the poetry of the headline

The news labels all uprisings
as riots instead of need

There is no easy way to step up
and say, "I demand to be free"

Mayors allow police to kill freely
and the President tells senators
who are Black to go home

I want to write in your baby book
that everything Baldwin wrote
was in between fires

a pause to breathe hope and fear
into chests

bellows for particular ends

Sugar from the Sun

My body produced you like a bee makes honey
    or like plants photosynthesize the sun

        IVF just an assist for forty-four year-old eggs
                that were born
                    in my mother's uterus

              you were always already
                      there

and the same would've been true
    even if my body hadn't produced

        I had already imagined our nights together
              snuggling on the couch

our weekends shopping at thrift stores
    so we could afford you

            you were already a smile across a diner booth
              and a dimple in a shared bed

there's so much I want to tell you about how
    the world works, but also I want you to stay sugar

            that I spun in my own web

I Am Working to Create Us a Home

of paper doll fantasies and cartoons
who are also animals and people

telling us about collective yearning
and the daily violence of obstacles

I am working to create us a home

in which the sounds of the lake amplify
our voices as we read your silly books

out loud to each other or practice noises
in the mirror where we see our lips move

I am working to create us a home

in a country of CEO bonuses
before laying off all the fast food cooks

I am working to create us a home

an apartment shielded by war poems
where we both know to acknowledge what is

I am working to create us a home

because a home is the best location
to craft jealousies for jealous neighbors

I am working to create us a home

and honestly I was kind of bored
with the profound lack of you around corners

so now there's this thing we do every
Monday through Sunday without any breaks

I am working to create us a home

I hope you like cause it's the only one
I can spin out of war and butterflies

Men Who Eat Ringforts

are the same as men who eat
my actions with their dead eyed
stares and flippant rolling mouths
at the edges of the universe
where the centuries unroll into
and out of my womb with only
lip service about my skills
at flattening a plan written
across a map on the top of a table
filled with pens and the drippings
of mustaches that have to be
swept aside to make way for
the world that is unrolling into
and out of the symbols that shift
even though they were once hard
data connected by synapses
and theories about how to win
against kings and their kingmakers
who are daily inventing new methods
to tally, grind, wax and wane
even if only on the head of a pin
where angels dance without sense
or vision simply to entertain
those who would place a heavy
creased thumb on their crowns

To My Daughter, In the Present

If I were to tell you just one thing
          in between the waves of pandemic
                    I would tell you "sand, political T-shirt, words born
of Holocaust and poverty, whole wheat scones"

          If I could tell you many, many things, I wouldn't
                              because your hair feels soft in my palm

I'm angry at everyone, but work
          to stabilize their homes

                         to keep the fairy tale winds and wolves
                                   sipping tea at the hearth

trading jokes about the stock market
          while three pigs reinforce with straw

                              when what we really need is no more
                                             straw
                                             or winds
                                             or wolves

or for straw to be enough

That would be the best way to tell you about the delays
          and the barricades and the

                         lack of everything we need at the exact time
                                             we need it

Better than telling you about mermaids
        without the voices they traded for legs

Or else that would be the best way
      of all the best ways
            because I want you to learn a woodpecker pecks
                a shoe makes a bad house

         and Jack is nimblest when he avoids the burn

the self of last year

moves through the weeds
of my body, unblinking
and unseen,
looking for water
where there is none

smells the dark
crawlspaces,
endlessly seeking
the blood-brain barrier
after a sudden
unexplained exile

not desperate
just hungry
for what it knows
in the way of all
grubbing foragers
lost

As We Move Through Erosions of Land and Economy

I'm at a loss for how to hold you better

                      so I know this is home

your smile a roving chandelier   among the pinecones

                  our bed a place to keep your laugh

      when not airing it out at the beach

         you jump into the watery divide

            dance shifting borders of sand meeting water

                  new delights and new terrors

     all the invisible edges rush to meet you

        in your simple acts

there are windows outside of us   a language spoken between two worlds

     when you say "something else"

          I know you mean "unutterable ecstasy of

        untold play"

          where someone else

            just hands you a ball

              or a new drink

they're not wrong, they just don't see all the other balls

            in existence

           but I do

                              but I do
when we look back into the night
        we see the list of names waiting for us
                        to say them:

                              bath
                              stars
                              book

            and we could be anywhere

                        the hearth of the
                        woods

                        the lip of our
                              space

Little one,

I want to tell you
of the hours.

The way my heart tolls
the years lost to moving
objects from one place
to another.

The bread-hands making.
The endless backlit
clicks and taps.

I used to read.

There are too many signs
and too many facial expressions.

I once stood on an overpass,
holding up the stars
I had pulled from the sky
and taped to a board,
spelling out the cold nights
of capitalism.

I had a brother
who told me to keep breathing
and writing and breathing
and writing.

I had a brother.

What more is there to do today?

Later I'm going to buy cupcakes

A lot of raids on families
have been thwarted by neighbors

People are finding they know how
to do the necessary things

I do laundry and turn on a stand-up
about single mothers

I laugh at men and their neediness
then read about 5 women shot

I wake up to announcements
about concentration camps,

facts denied, and a looming fiery
death from the sun

I put furniture close to the ground
in my daughter's room,
hang a picture of a fox

Origin Stories

you pull yourself up by the ledge

       the window, windless
    holds you above a scene

         trees, cars, passersby

               The Shadow and Finger
                 of the Almighty
          a store front church next to taquerias

         the worse the advertising and
             ambience, the better the food

      I read about Greenland
             proving people live there

    enough to spawn *Arctic Today*
         cities with nightclubs and traditions

            stories of a hungry goddess
        clinging to a boat until she sinks

    after her creator chops off
       fingers that become whales

            so many origin stories and
       sciences of reproduction

I'm lucky to have conceived you
        without going to Embryoland
            a medical tourist in Greece

                how will I explain to you some day
                    the various circles

           the beauty of a metaphor
             and also the harm

teach you a critical mind
      and keen appreciation for subtlety

         wind blowing through leaves
           across the receptors of your soft skin

April 14, 2020

Chicago's beach is empty of people
and filled with pigeons

The blue lake creates a postcard
backdrop to your swing

No children running the playground
just empty bottle caps and peanuts

We have this time to ourselves
during what should be the work day

What should be entire work weeks

You run ahead to walk concrete
ledges like balance beams

Your hand is small and warm
when I hold it on the high parts

At the Heart of Everything

I go to the park because it's warm and I'm alive. Walking there is a statement I make after the winter. I've been sitting in the dark hole of the couch, watching Taylor sing "Betty" and hitting replay on the beacon of her smile.

I didn't realize a million people were going to die. Now my toddler and I are sitting at an outdoors café again, and she asks where the birdhouse is. I don't understand how a two-and-a-half-year-old brain can remember such a small detail. A week is forever, but she knows to look for a tiny house in a tree.

I present on escalating actions for workers. I want to tell them my favorite sound is "Mommy" and that I've been squeezing out my heart over and over. That at night, I dive into *Normal People*, *Atlanta*, and Bridgers's "Moon Song." Search out Oberst's most recent drunken performances, tumble down Kaylor and Maylor rabbit holes.

I construct birdhouses to line the path from my past to the future. Things come to roost.

Baby, today I'm mad.

The beach is our neighbor. There's sand everywhere and lots of room for people, but the worship has gone.

How do I tell you sky is vault and the color blue is organ? My voice must be majestic to make this case for you.

Or maybe not. Maybe the particularity of grains is enough. Maybe the mass politics of waves echoes through the space all around us. It's harder to demonstrate the relationship between particles and trees, between energy and matter, than it is to be them.

In this way, you can have your empty church with a dirt floor swept clean of debris and your soaring stained glass windows gleaming near the cathedral rafters, both.

Because nothing can fuck up space.

something lifted

some rock or fire

some backchannel conversation
the evidence of which now moving through the gorge
on full display

God, don't let me forget the filthy carpet
and the holes in the wall
but also don't let them stay

it's a spiral, it's a gas
underneath the stars
we're spinning out

how much time is left
to explore the gap between now and now

not the effluvia
of pain, a childhood falling to pieces
like leftover Christmas trees in the alley

but instead forest and filth
your moon face and apple cheeks

no one said the particles would be
screaming, no one said adults
would be pool sharks at life

How Do I Tell You Where I Come From?

When you'll be more like the girls
                    I thought I hated

the ones who were two-story houses with garages
                                        and five pairs of jeans

                            Will loving me be enough

to see the food stamp weather   moving across my geography
            roaches crawling inside my mouth
                                and my books all falling open
to no nights at the dollar show

        When my eyelids close, will you see a film projected
                of an engine
                        hoisted up on a chain slung over a tree branch

                        a body slinking out of a red Vega
                            with a scavenged orange hood

                            trying not to be seen
                                    at the high school

Will you hear the waves in my ears
            pounding my mother's untreated yeast infections
                into a lyric

                    and my brother's payday loans
                        and my other brother's jail stints
                            and

Or will I have to show you the poem
that says

> "I was the maid's room
> pretending not to know the gratuitous
> nature of the maid's room
> my own mother, a kitchen"

then leave you to your best guesses
and any homework you give yourself
to puzzle out where you fit in the poem that ends

"and we rise slowly"

II.

Groceries. Beer. Liquor. Lottery.

My date studies geography, but not boring geography, hot geography. The kind where they figure the ratio of Jesus to horses.

There's always a ratio. Jesus to horses. Highschools to Speedways. Liquor to lottery.

All landscape makes me sad. There are always people picnicking near the pond at the end of the park, and all I can think is it's too far to walk just to sit on a blanket.

The people reading in chairs tire me, too—How do they manage to be so relaxed? Does it require a lifetime of practice?—while the whiteness of vans in the sun echoes through the parking lot.

Those lines in the lawn become wavy near the lot. As if to make a point. And yet patterns are neither just plans nor just accidents.

For instance, my teenage brothers stole and stole and stole until every TV was a replacement for the one just used to buy smokes.

Insurgent

It didn't matter that we couldn't afford
all the electric bills that made light

I did my homework romantically
I did my dodgy life by candlelight

A child who didn't know not to play
with her grandpa's war-given glass eyes

A practitioner of the retrograde arts
The unimagined girl in the backdrop

I watched men in waders fishing in weeds
magically pulling fish from the grass

I rode in a car with a red body
and an orange hood salvaged from junk

I learned all the things that shouldn't go
I was the girl doing kerosene math

Three Object Lessons: The Serving Girl

i.

By '79, I was a piano
someone else's place to put sheets
I was stupid back then about refusing
the moths beating in the window, a worry
all those gloves, crumpled, on the foyer
a piece about the migration of birds
while I held up vases, *that* kind of music

ii.

so many pretty, tired boys asking
handouts, reacharounds, start smiling at 2:00

how they fixed things was the tea things
kept disappearing until *not that much*

iii.

I was the maid's room, pretending not to know
the gratuitous nature of the maid's room
my own mother, a kitchen

Beauties necessary and unnecessary

the trees look greener in foodstamp season
and our stomachs are composed
of spider webs with sunlight on them

I've been whetting my hunger all day
on the strop of your abundance
while the beautiful chain gang
that is my family
runs the streets

their discord is a symphony
waking us all from bluebird reveries

and we rise slowly

When Your Brother, Who Is in Jail Again

—a poem written from myself to myself

when your brother calls to say his fists are turning into thieves
             and your niece is a sweet collection of thrushes and wrens

             you should take notes so that you can understand the curve
                                                                  of his reasoning

you must accept that indeed you come from a long line of wounds

             return to your village and open up The Book of the Mumbling Dead

reading is
your last good way of saying your name without it hurting

             your name: *all the flowers that are edible*

                              after all you come from a line of chefs

                                   open to the page lined with
                                        there are always
                                        already and only
                                        three true outcomes:

       the fox to the hare, the splinter to the sea, and the unsure thing

eventually you will understand the voices of the sand in the rocks
and theorize houses as an attraction of bricks

                    there are so many things that don't make sense

         like the timid girls wandering onto the private beach
like your body, irresolute and shaped by food

if you can accept your deceased
     pulling their chairs up to your table to eat
         if you can accept the rain as just another pattern happening

         you can begin to indent your belief

after all you come from the sea

The Plebs

The plebs were laughed. Were, much more clearly, my mother, gaping.

Years earlier, they were all laughing. Were the sexual allusions of one who has a role. The metal dealer. The Waiters. That fight for vulgar toasts. When who should be served dirty against my father's shoulder.

While he, who had drunk wine, was now the expression of food and wine, his mouth, increasingly serious. And leaning, knew what the plebs were when the plebs clattered. Even Lila, first and better than at that quarrel over who should play the plebs.

And I will be it to the utmost at that moment. Me, that floor on which she had asked, back and forth.

First Footing

a child carrying flowers walks toward the new year

a dragon with a blood red tongue lashes out at passersby

friends throw their dishes at your door as a sign of kinship

how many chairs will your brother leap over tonight

the run from the police is filled with untold obstacles

twelve steps move you toward yourself in the future

a GED moves you away from a motel and eight an hour

all first guests should be male and enter carrying coal

all knives should be hidden so there are no accidents

the frugality of black-eyed peas will protect us

sacrificial boats filled with jewelry launch from the shore

Descending a Staircase

I'm becoming scared of the moon.

My bones are drawn forward
on a tide, and the creak
won't drain from my ear.

I go to the doctor.
I ask him to take away
what I hear.

I go to the doctor.
I ask her to tell stories
to my knees.

There's a meanness inside.

Maybe if we light a candle
it can be smoked out my nose.

No one listens to my ideas.
They say I'm all fetish
and pin-pricked dolls.

And I guess I am becoming communal.

I used to feel just like
a private party.

Now my pubic hair softens
the floor of every room.

III.

Carnage

holy, holy, holy
instrumental score
for a film
about that ruffian Jesse James

how did such sounds make
their way
into my head
to reflect the shape of both
the hole that was left
in me
and the sky and the sun and the waves
that were all
I could see
when I looked
up from looking
at the hole-shaped shape of me

I kept wanting to fight
it
I kept wanting to fight

it was so far down
to the ground
and yet suddenly there
the ground was

I gave myself up

for a few minutes

I was a person
bathed in sunlight

IV.

Bodies, Useful and Celebratory

I surprised myself by giving orders
                and my friends squeezed across the floor
                                bodies recruiting bodies
a warm sweating everywhere
                until there were bodies
                        mapped with sandwich and water routes
and we had to sustain the cities of changing bodies
                                    because this wasn't formal
                because the exits and elevators kept multiplying
but we were going to break this Wisconsin budget
                through a quorum of kindergarten teachers
                      and soon this would be set to Arcade Fire
a video of my friends at the doors   laughing and leading their groups
        but first the thousands had birthed us
                              none of us could claim it
least of all the critics roaming freely outside
                    while we made ourselves sick with our cities
the work it takes to keep politicians inside
                to keep moving bodies risky and focused

Eventually We Will All

Eventually we will all be doing what we want to be doing. Magazines and horoscopes say so.

I fear my body. The way it's crisscrossed with maps and struggles with location.

Men in khaki shorts and Cubs hats surround us in the otherwise free zone known as Damen Ave.

Soon I won't be able to afford a car, because it's always getting towed.

Invisible electric fences follow us wherever we go, our bodies constituting foreign trade zones.

There's a skate park under the overpass. I know some kids who love freedom.

We ask for water in tall glasses. The water is free, and the tallness seems a luxury.

I am always just exiting Regal Cinemas, wishing I could go back to the show.

Only in chaos are we conceivable

i.
I miss sadness

the cloud forest

the chemical library
of my own nostalgia

the drums of Calanda
moving closer
in my dreams

ii.
the weight of something
that was you
confusing me about my own
animalness

until I could no longer identify
nails, teeth
they were buried so deeply
in my flesh

iii.
now I have
resentment
at the type of privilege
that gave birth
to "pulp-free"

this strange pacing
thing
making plans
inside me

Rue

To be at right angle to the river simply to keep a shapely line is to misunderstand the reason for building. Boulevards end in climax: the discipline of columns. Several avenues converging on an opera house is a watchful eye in a city where the rues are merely tactical. Revolution, a sympathy between dark windows. A street built for parades will eventually terminate in slums. Classical? Put your cupola to its purpose. The citizens will want a public market. But under colored awnings, Paris is still a military camp. Lanterns smashing, horses freed – only an emperor would build streets of muddy macadam even when told the people had no stilts. Who would ever want to go from the Bourse to the Opera? A magistrate once dangled from the streetlamp at Hotel de Ville. A lack of shortcomings will stir no blood.

May Day

My mouth is crowded with weather
                              left over from today's parade.
What will grow here out of the fist
            waving on a flag I reached to touch
                              with my fingers while a boy watched?
                                          Will it look
like a woman standing on a car with a camera?
                              Did she catch our faces right?
Will viewers see us singing *Clandestino!* at the ends of lines
            in between buying food from a truck
and watching red-winged blackbirds?
                              I want to know what kind of erotica
the Subcomandate writes.
                        Surely he knows how to write sunburned eyes
and how to make Lorca kiss Mayakovsky next to the elote cart.
                        And also how to make them just another thing happening
while all those feet march the streets and sidewalks.
            While the band plays music
                        until the confusion of birds and traffic is hot.
We have to be where we're at
                              because in the Midwest there is no horizon.
The water around this city   is the kind of fluid doctors talk about.
                              We create spectacle, our bodies moving
into a future filled with vendors who sell nothing,
                                          barter in moments.
I open my coat: a Milwaukee street like a Paris committee,
                        a protester like a laptop in a forest.

Dear Mike Davis,

L.A. is still a mess   its people divided by tax lines and highways

      the census taker reinforces at their doorstep

            because there is no version—
                    of life
                    or story or art or
                    ways of preparing
                    food
                    that comes stuffed
                    into tin—

            that doesn't involve taxonomy and oppression

How much worse

         if it weren't for all those high school walk outs

                      by anonymous brown
        teenagers

I had to learn about in a bookstore in the back

         of a dress shop in East L.A.

         So much harder to come by than "Tippecanoe and Tyler

too," which my gym/history teacher

        taught sleepy students in Southern Illinois

movie poem

if socialism is equality
then I am that, too,
as well as a mother birthing
myself as my own mother-
daughter, but not without
also being birthed by context,
which is to say all that is around
including, sometimes, you,
even the violence of you,
because no one is without flaws
of the sort that birth a man
acting as a goat, testing his man-
goat teeth on the edges of lawns
for my pleasure and his safe-
keeping, which is to say, yes,
I saw that movie, too, and it hit
brain and bone, so now I am both
daughter-mother birthing my
self and birthing my goat-man
who is maybe a part of me
I'd like to keep tethered
nearby, so I put him here for safe-
keeping in this poem that is movie,
but also my hands typing me/you

Clutching a Pole in Norway

"The greatest tragedy that can befall us is to go unimagined."
— N. Scott Momaday

In this film, a reindeer girl hangs on in incredible wind. In this film, a speaker narrates the lives of the Sami, Norway's native peoples. In this film, sculptures of wood and fire line the edge of a lake and burn back history.

Shifting borders are lifted and lit. Suspended in the lit air: Norwegians, Finnish, Russians.

Ice sculptures either make or undo themselves over candles. (The perspective is yours.) What isn't yours – the designs of crepe paper, dipped in water, frozen.

In an incredible wind, a reindeer girl hangs on, and I'm imagining her breathing.

Terror

my neighbor's missing teeth   those blank pages

                    a thirty-foot white cross looming in the rearview mirror

I keep trying to find new words for this must-be-disease

          the difficulty of shitting in jail

                                        there are no keystrokes

          here are all the shivering testicles

                    coughing nights on the Wisconsin capitol's floors

                                        I once knew how to use verbs

the leafy redness that terrorizes from gardens and vases

                                        an inward branching

Simone composing, swelling with "Mississippi Goddamn"

How Widespread Do You Think Your Support Is?

I like the stranger bits of vacation.
Like people farting in Sacre Couer.

Like flirting couples touching and posing
and being shushed in Sacre Couer.

Like writing interview questions for striking
workers while sitting in the prayer section.

Like pressing knee to pew, pencil to paper
in Sacre Couer, the questions a prayer.

Like fingering the hunk of bread in my bag
that needs to get me through this journey.

Like shivering in a jacket while the mist
covers the graffiti and the churches

and the protesters gently hugging flares
to be lit later in the train station.

Recognition

guards treat the pizzeros
like flunkeys convalescing in the hot sun   or a bacterial picket line,
        one-celled and multiplying
a heel-to-toe phantasm on the sidewalk
       police threatening citations   for stepping on the grass
        backstepping through history
until strikers and allies fight back through Instagram
        a strategic nostalgia for sweating
           letterboxed for the news
    El pueblo unido . . .
       the language of missing fingers   parading through living rooms
people need to know   we are all loopy survivalists of realism
          and there are circles
forming right now under the sun

Week Twelve

women are handing out tampons in Albany Park

people are driving around joyfully
      mass redistributing TVs

The McDonald's is boarded up
      and the trains aren't running

         there isn't a sound anywhere
         writes one woman online, holed up
            in Rogers Park, itself holed up

in a world of multi-day multi-city "riots"

I have love for the redistributors

while the mayors
        stop trains
     and stop free school lunches
        and stop breath

     I have my thumbprint all over strikes

but right now I'm cooking dinner
      after a trip to the park with my daughter
wearing masks to stop viral spread

           various demographics are trying
              in various ways not to die

isolated and still
striking
looting and burning

people are maybe still singing from balconies
and banging pots with spoons

V.

Carnage

Wrought, wrought, wrought
like the soil underneath
when the blade digs in

the grind of religion and
the 7:30 am stop for coffee
and the political treatise
on the front lawn and
under the car's wipers
while the brain keeps grinding
out the conversation

your mother doesn't remember
that moment in history
when everyone stood up

and your child moves through
history like a whirlwind
made of many smaller
versions of herself

let go of the clear, clean

you have to see that no one
can see through your eyes
and that all you make
is an homage to what could be

you have to be in love with
the opening in the future

when you all march through
chanting that thing together

even once you return to
the Tuesdays and the meat
slices between bread
the floaters always hovering
in your field of vision
the backwards tumble into
the ravine and the muddy
stupid footprints on whatever
thing you just bought

Epilogue

Take One, Take Two, Take Three

1:

I want to know my own face
in each of the rooms.
Already faces there, looking
like someone no one imagined,
like no one's idea of a good time,
or a strike won, or a line
that grabs you by the throat,
or even a just a slow swing
in a hammock in the breeze.
Birds hanging around
singing the kinds of songs
that birds sing, cake
with funfetti sprinkles,
and lithographs of the original
anti-fascist man in a cap.
All the chairs are already taken
and a chorus of high school
girls starts whispering.
It's probably time to sit down,
but some witch not exactly
hiding casts a spell
less about knowing than feeling
ones way through a room.

2:

I want to know each of the rooms.
Looking like someone,
like no one's idea of a strike won,
or birds hanging around in the breeze.
I want to be the original lithograph
of the anti-fascist man in a cap,
funfetti sprinkles,
a chorus of high school girls.
It's probably time to cast a spell
less about knowing than feeling
ones way through a room.

3:

I want to know
someone,
a chorus of girls,
a strike won,
birds hanging around in the breeze.
To be the original
anti-fascist man in a cap,
funfetti sprinkles,
a way through a room.

Acknowledgements

Grateful acknowledgment is made to the editors of those publications in which versions of the following poems originally appeared:

Bennington Review: "Three Object Lessons: The Serving Girl"

Birdcoat Quarterly: "When I Win, I Start Again"

BlazeVOX: "Eventually We Will All"; "When Your Brother, Who Is in Jail Again"

Concision Poetry Magazine: "How Do I Tell You Where I Come From?"

decomP: "L&D"

Denver Quarterly: "Descending a Staircase"

Fence: "Only in chaos are we conceivable"

great weather for MEDIA: "The Ongoing Work of Liberation, Or the Aggressiveness of Liberation Theology"

Interim: "As We Move Through Erosions of Land and Economy"; "Home / Shelter / View"

Kestrel: "Carnage"

Mudlark: "At the Heart of Everything"; "Beauties necessary and unnecessary"; "Carnage"; "How Widespread Do You Think Your Support Is?"; "Little one"; "My Daughter Sleeps with the Lights Dimmed"; "Nashville's Court House Is Burning"

Pangyrus: "To My Daughter, In the Present"

Sequestrum: "Men Who Eat Ringforts"; "Take One, Take Two, Take Three"

Verse Wisconsin: "Bodies, Useful and Celebratory"; "May Day"; "Recognition"

Witness: "Clutching a Pole in Norway"; "Groceries. Beer. Liquor. Lottery

About the Author

Dawn Tefft's poems appear in *Denver Quarterly*, *Fence*, and *Witness*. Her chapbooks include *Gosling* (Anhinga Press), *Fist* (Dancing Girl Press), and *Field Trip to My Mother and Other Exotic Locations* (Mudlark). She earned a PhD in English at University of Wisconsin-Milwaukee and volunteers as an editor for *Packingtown Review*. She works as a union representative in Chicago, where she raises the most wonderful child and enjoys life-affirming friendships.

www.ingramcontent.com/pod-product-compliance
Lightning Source LLC
Chambersburg PA
CBHW051329120626
46547CB00016B/2467